CHRISTCHURCH PRIORY

CHRISTCHURCH PRIORY

BENJAMIN POLK

AE ACADEMY EDITIONS

BENJAMIN POLK is an American architect and planner whose personal design practice has been largely in south Asia. Among his important works are the great Buddhist Tripitaka Library in Rangoon, the Royal Palace for His Majesty the King of Nepal, Kathmandu, and the beautiful Jallianwala Bagh Memorial in Amritsar, along with university and college groups, museums and theatres, as well as extensive industrial, apartment, business and residential buildings.

Publications by Benjamin Polk include *Architecture and the Spirit of the Place*, Rupa, 1961; with Emily Polk, *India Notebook*, Arts & Architecture Press, Santa Monica, 1986; and *Building for South Asia*, Abhinav Publications, New Delhi, 1993. The Polks were resident in England for ten years – 1981-91.

ACKNOWLEDGEMENT
The great experiences of Gothic architecture with its many archaeological challenges came to me first in England as I analysed the small, beautiful Wiltshire churches at Bishopstone and Steeple Ashton. The privilege of living in England for those ten years cannot be adequately spelled out, and the many friendships formed especially in the Salisbury and Christchurch areas are lasting ones – both for myself and my wife. We wish to acknowledge all the generosities we received during that splendid time.

Cover: Plan of Christchurch Priory, Dorset

Historical Monograph
Editorial Office: 42 Leinster Gardens London W2 3AN

Series Editor: Michael Spens
Art Editor: Andrea Bettella
Editorial and Design Team: Mark Lane, David Rosie

First published in Great Britain in 1994 by
ACADEMY EDITIONS
An imprint of the Academy Group Ltd

ACADEMY GROUP LTD
42 Leinster Gardens London W2 3AN
Member of the VCH Publishing Group

ISBN 1 85490 382 9

Distributed to the trade in the United States of America by
ST MARTIN'S PRESS
175 Fifth Avenue, New York, NY 10010

Origination and printing organised by Book Production Consultants Plc, Cambridge
Printed and bound in the United Kingdom

CONTENTS

PREFACE

Christchurch Priory in Dorset[1] has intrigued both architects and scholars for over two hundred years. Evidence of this fascination is clear enough in the attentions of some twenty-six authors. Archaeological methods have guided much of their research, and nineteenth century architectural amendments may have revealed more than they confused fresh study. Even Pevsner was unable to resolve outstanding questions of origin and date concerning areas of the fabric of a building, once known as England's longest parish church, and longer than some cathedrals.

Christchurch was fortunate to be planned by the famous Ranulf Flambard and started under his guidance in 1094. However, this leading cleric, who was already Dean of St Paul's Cathedral in London, fell out of favour with the new King Henry I, and went out of circulation for a period, before, significantly, he became Bishop of Durham and built that great cathedral. Ben Polk traces evidence of such linkages in exploring the stages of change and development at Christchurch, which provided a clear basis for the church's future development in many and varied ways.

The advantage the author has here over his predecessors in the assessment and analysis of Christchurch is that he combines scholarly research, spread over a ten-year period, with the fruits of a lifetime in architectural practice. He is therefore well enabled to synthesise, in his approach to the resolution, the 'riddles' of Christchurch. Polk does not lose sight of the whole architecture while exploring the details.

This is a first in a series of monographs to explore a number of single historical, important buildings that merit re-appraisal by various authors. Such architectural examples exist in every period, from the prehistoric to the contemporary, when there is a clear relevance to architectural design, adaptations over time, interpretation of changing requirements and visual significance and meaning.

At Christchurch, as Ben Polk clearly shows, it is the evolutionary process of adaptation and change over several centuries, and a corresponding sustenance of religious meaning through such adaptation, that places it firmly within such criteria for student and practitioner alike.   *Michael Spens*

[1] *Other commentators have referred to the site of Christchurch Priory as being in Hampshire; however, the planning department of Dorset County Council has confirmed that the site is presently in Dorset.*

HISTORY AND DATES

To introduce the facts I shall partially quote publications by the Priory itself, reserving the right to amplify, modify and omit.

The building of the *present* Christchurch Priory was started in 1094 during the reign of William Rufus, third son of William the Conqueror. It was planned by Ranulf Flambard who held high office under the King and owned a manor in the New Forest. He was Dean of St Paul's Cathedral, London, but, after Rufus died in a hunting incident near Christchurch, fell foul of King Henry I and was banished from the Kingdom for a short while. When he returned, he became Bishop of Durham and built there the great cathedral which bears some features comparable with the Priory.

It is interesting to conjecture whether the Priory of Christchurch might have been wholly completed in the Norman style of architecture had Flambard not been forced to leave Christchurch only six years after he had begun building it. Durham Cathedral became the greatest masterpiece of Romanesque architecture in Europe. It was virtually completed in the space of forty years. The building of the Priory spread over four and a half centuries.

An outline of historical events during the forty reigns in which the Priory has existed, vividly portrays the great age and significance of this, the longest parish church in England.

The Priory is larger than several English Cathedrals. It includes excellent examples of all the principal styles of architecture from early Norman, which evolved during the period of four hundred years in which the building was created.

The architectural styles of the interior can be classified as Norman (1093/94 to 1190), nave and transepts, Early Gothic (1190 to 1300), north nave aisle and north porch, Decorated Gothic (1300 to

1400), south nave aisle windows, the choir and Jesse screen, Perpendicular (1400 to 1520), choir, Lady Chapel and tower, and Renaissance (1520), Salisbury and Draper Chantries.

The Priory formed part of what became, prior to the Dissolution in the 1530s, one of the country's larger monasteries. The first prior was appointed in 1150 and it was only because of the pleading of the last prior, John Draper, that the church itself was spared in 1539 from the destruction of the English monasteries, which took place during the reign of King Henry VIII.

North Porch

The very large entrance to the church dates from the late twelfth century. This was where the prior met burgesses to transact such business as tolls and tithes. Certain services are also thought to have been held there.

A most interesting feature of the porch is the wide-spreading and deeply recessed pointed arch with its two doors forming the direct entrance to the church.

Nave

Typically Norman piers and rounded arches are to be seen here, which, together with the original choir beyond the screen and the two transepts, were the first parts of the church to be built.

The site on which Flambard started to build was earlier occupied by a Saxon church of which only very little remains in one of the crypts. (Augustine had brought Christianity to the south coast more than four hundred and fifty years before the Norman conquest.)

Above the main arches another series of smaller arches is the triforium, so called because the comparable Norman arcades at Canterbury have triple openings towards the nave. Higher still is the clerestory added to provide light to the upper part of the interior.

The regular pattern of carving in the space between the rounded arches (the spandrel) was carved with the hatchet as, at that time, the chisel was not in common use for carving.

Within the nave, one is confronted with one of the finest vistas of Norman architecture to be seen anywhere in the Kingdom. The screen at the far end (which supported the rood-loft before the Reformation) was added later, but the massive piers of clustered columnar form are original Norman work.

South Nave Aisle

On the west, the rounded arches originally opened to the cloisters, which occupied a large square on the south side of the church.

Surrounding the cloisters, on three sides, were the other conventual buildings of the Priory where the community of the religious order lived and worked until their buildings were destroyed during the reign of Henry VIII.

In the early days, all the religious celebrations took place in the choir, on the east side of the stone screen. No seating was provided in the nave, which quite often would provide a meeting place for the local populace, as well as offering them the opportunity of worship. The low seat running along the south wall of the aisle is typical of early churches and doubtless gives an origin of the saying 'the weak go to the wall'.

Crossing and Transepts

(Plates 30 and 37.) Standing at the corner of the screen, one can see part of the beautiful timbered roof which actually extends over the entire length of the nave. The plaster vaulting, hiding most of it, was added in Victorian times possibly to help to conserve the heating of the nave.

The detailed fourteenth century carvings on the screen are delightful. Notice the variety of little animals gambolling in pairs just above eye level. Note, particularly, the one isolated example of what the old sculptor did when he ran out of 'animal' ideas. Was it his own face he carved? Look for the beautiful carvings of acorns, including the one empty cup, and the superb bunches of grapes at the north end of the screen. This screen, or 'pulpitum', sharply divides the nave from the choir and, indeed, was put in for that very purpose. With a growing local population, the nave would increasingly be used by the public. The screen would help to seclude the choir for the celebration of the many religious offices.

In fact, this screen and the 'Jesse' screen to the east clearly mark the existence in the Priory of three separate churches. Each has its own altar – three remaining from the nine with which the Priory is said to have been furnished at the beginning of the thirteenth century.

Originally, both of the transepts were divided into two storeys. The small iron railing along the north wall marks a narrow passage joining series of steps inside the walls by which access is gained to a 'cat-walk' above the centre of the nave vaulting.

South Choir Aisle

On the north side of the aisle are the chantry chapel of Robert Harys, one-time vicar of Christchurch, and the entrance to the chancel crypt, now the vault of the Malmesbury family. On the south side is the choir vestry. At the end, against the east wall is the chapel of the last prior, John Draper, and, in front of it, his tombstone which was moved from the nave in 1840. Above the entrance to the chapel is a carving depicting the initials 'JD' and a representation of a church with a central tower, one of several in the church to lend weight to the conviction that there was originally a central tower which fell and destroyed the choir.

Lady Chapel

Here are beautiful examples of early Perpendicular windows and, behind the altar, a much restored reredos which dates from the mid-fifteenth century.

North Choir Aisle

As you leave the Lady Chapel look back at the legendary 'miraculous beam' of the Priory. The story of this remarkable relic is displayed on the easel nearby. Certain it is that some event occurred which caused the name of the place to be changed from 'Twynham' (from the Saxon for 'between the rivers') to Christchurch. And certain it is that the high altar, the table[1] of which was designed by AW Pugin at the tender age of nineteen (1831), in the great choir was dedicated to Christ. (At the present time, the Priory is dedicated to the Holy Trinity.)

In the north aisle is the tomb bearing the alabaster figures of Sir John and Lady Chideoke. Sir John was killed in battle during the Wars of the Roses.

Notice, on the left, the steps worn by countless pilgrims leading to the Salisbury Chantry and, beyond the steps which lead to the great choir, the chantry chapel of Sir William Berkeley (1486) showing the original painted decoration of red and white roses. This marked the end of the Wars of the Roses with the accession of Henry VII and the Union of the Tudor red rose with the white rose of York when he married Elizabeth of York, daughter of Edward IV.

Great Choir

(Plate 11.) Rebuilt after destruction by the fallen tower, this part of the church preserves the ancient monks' stalls bearing a variety of carvings which recorded facts and commentaries at the time (see the representation of the fox, cowled as a friar, preaching to a flock of geese). Another very famous carving portrays King Richard III.

In the great screen there is another story in stone – that of the genealogy of Christ stemming, as a vine, from the side of Jesse and showing the Holy Family and three Kings bringing gifts. Above this are the ox and the ass and three shepherds on the hill with their goats and sheep.

Here is the chantry chapel of Margaret, Countess of Salisbury, daughter of the Duke of Clarence, who reputedly was drowned in a butt of Malmsey wine in the Tower of London. At one time a court favourite of Henry VIII, Margaret was given the manor of Christchurch. Married to the great grandson of Geoffrey Chaucer, Sir Richard Pole, their son Reginald was training for the priesthood in Rome where he fiercely attacked the religious policies of the King. Being unable to reach his son and in pursuance of his fanatical hunt for Yorkist blood, Henry vented his spleen on his former favourite, Reginald's ageing mother, the last of the Plantagenets. He threw her into the Tower of London in 1539 and ordered her execution two years later. Her body never rested in this her chantry. Carved on the outside wall is the *'Plante à Genista'* (Plantagenet).

Her son, Reginald, became a cardinal, papal delegate to Mary Tudor and Archbishop of Canterbury. He was buried in Canterbury Cathedral.

West End

Here are the Books of Remembrance and the chapel dedicated to those who lost their lives in two World Wars and, facing the christening font, is the memorial to the English poet Shelley drowned off the coast of Italy in 1822.

[1] *The High Altar table is described as 'a small oak table with five bat front, the bays of three different widths being filled with flamboyant open work vine trails and other worthy shapes.' (Pevsner,* The Buildings of England, Hampshire, *under Christchurch Priory.)*

THE PRIORY DURING TWENTY-THREE REIGNS

Only when the known history of Christchurch Priory is set side-by-side with events in the story of England since the Norman Conquest, and related to other changes in the local scene, can the great age of the church be fully appreciated.

CONTEMPORARY HISTORY		LOCAL HISTORY	
	WILLIAM THE CONQUEROR 1066-1087		
1086	Domesday Book		
	WILLIAM RUFUS 1087-1100		
	Flambard Dean of St Paul's Cathedral, London	1093/ 1094	Flambard began building Priory Church
1099	Bishop of Durham		
	HENRY I 1100-1135		
1100	Flambard imprisoned in Tower of London, escaped to Normandy		Roof partly completed. Transepts built. Christchurch Castle being built
1107	Flambard returned to Durham (d 1128)		
	STEPHEN 1135-1154		
		1140	A school first attached to Priory (continued until 1869)
		1150	The first prior appointed
	HENRY II 1154-1189		
1167	First English University at Oxford		Triforium added

1170 Archbishop Becket murdered	1160 Constable's House built
1176/	
1209 London Bridge built	
1182 Francis of Assisi born (d 1226)	

RICHARD I 1189-1199
(HE SPENT NO MORE THAN FIVE MONTHS IN ENGLAND)

Geoffrey Plantagenet, illegitimate son of Henry II, became Bishop of Lincoln at age of 14 and Archbishop of York at 21	Nave roof completed (at triforium level) High Altar in choir consecrated

JOHN I 1199-1216

1208/	
1214 England under Papal Interdict	1200 Aisles vaulted
1209 The King is excommunicated	1214 Nave altar consecrated
1214 Roger Bacon born	
1215 Magna Carta	

HENRY III 1216-1272

1221 Friars land in England	1220 Oldest misericord seat carved
1249 First college founded at Oxford	1230 North nave aisle windows
1254 Marco Polo born (d 1323)	1250 Second oldest misericord carved

EDWARD I 1272-1307
(LORD OF THE MANOR OF TWYNHAM)

1306 Rising of Robert the Bruce	Clerestory completed. North Porch started

EDWARD II 1307-1327

Papacy abandoned Rome and settled in Avignon	1308 Christchurch invited to send two members to Parliament, but pleaded too poor to do so
	1317 First endowment of local Leper Hospital
	1320 Choir screen put in

EDWARD III 1327-1377

1340 Chaucer born (d 1400)	1350 Jesse reredos carved
1346 Battle of Crécy	1370 Two earliest bells cast.
1348/	Nave roofed? Lady Chapel
1349 The Black Death	started

RICHARD II 1377-1399

Wyclif (b 1328 d 1384)   1390   Lady Chapel completed
translated Bible into English

HENRY IV 1399-1413

Revolt of Owen Glendower

HENRY V 1413-1422

Battle of Agincourt

HENRY VI 1422-1461

Death of Joan of Arc   Choir rebuilt
Kings College Chapel started   Lady Chapel vaulted and
Leonardo da Vinci born (d 1519)   screen built
Wars of the Roses   1435   First recorded Mayor of
End of 100 Years' Wars with   Christchurch
France   1460   Tomb of Sir John and Lady
                                                         Chideoke installed

EDWARD IV 1461-1483

Copernicus born (d 1543)   Present choir started?
Michelangelo born (d 1564)   West tower added
Caxton brought printing to
England
Titian born (d 1576)

EDWARD V 1483 (MURDERED)

RICHARD III 1483-1485

HENRY VII 1485-1509

Columbus discovered America   1486   Berkeley Chantry built
Vasco da Gama's sea route to   Present choir completed. In
India   general appearance, the
Colet and Erasmus at Oxford   church has reached the state
Francis I of France born (d 1547)   in which it stands today
Reginald Pole born (d 1558)

HENRY VIII 1509-1547

Sir Thomas More's *Utopia*	1520	Prior Draper elected
Luther denounces indulgences	1538	Cromwell's Commissioners at
Pope awards King title, Defender		the Priory
of the Faith	1539	Priory surrendered to the
Tyndal translates Bible		King
Wolsey died, replaced by	1540	(23 Oct) Church granted to
Thomas Cromwell		inhabitants and
Henry VIII, head of Church		churchwardens
in England		as their parish church
More executed	1541	Beheading of Margaret,
Reading of Bible in English		Countess of Salisbury,
first permitted		granddaughter of Warwick
Destruction of shrines of Edward		the Kingmaker, last of the
the Confessor and Thomas Becket		Plantagenets, mother of
		Reginald Pole and Lady of the
		manor of Twynham. She was
		nearly 70 when executed

EDWARD VI 1547-1553

Cranmer's Prayer Book in	1522	Prior Draper died
English		
Second Book of Common Prayer		

MARY 1553-1558

Cardinal Pole returned to	Church reverted to Rome
England; made Archbishop of	during Mary's reign
Canterbury	
Archbishop Cranmer burnt	
Archbishop Pole died	
(within a few hours of Queen)	

ELIZABETH I 1558-1603

	Slave trade with Africa begins	
1571	Thirty-nine Articles evolved	1571 Christchurch first sent
	William Shakespeare born	members regularly to
	(d 1616)	Parliament
	Galileo born (d 1642)	
	Defeat of the Armada	
	Velázquez born (d 1660)	

INTRODUCTION TO THE RESEARCH

By evaluating the frame of mind of the architects of one of the great medieval churches one might be able to shed new light on both aesthetic and archaeological matters. This should be true of Christchurch Priory, Dorset, with its several construction stops and starts and its abrupt changes of plan over its nine hundred years of development.

Much design with its implied detail was well understood by the churchmen and the masons, as well as by the architects in those days. Although many design decisions were 'inner-directed', that is they came as creative decisions by the architects, many decisions were 'outer-directed' by the client or by the necessary limits of equipment, materials, funds, etc. Often the unspoken way ahead was simply perceived by all concerned.

Romanesque and Gothic architecture were by no means vague or undefined, but in the decades of the late eleventh, twelfth and thirteenth centuries the power of God (as in Psalm 96, for example) was felt by our ancestors as an everyday experience, and they believed it worked for His glory in architecture. The human and intellectual achievement of design and construction, stupendous as it was, was seen in detail to be a part of God's universal purpose. These were centuries of splendid architectural opportunities, not of 'design problems'. The world was young. Christianity was implicit *and* explicit and gave a purpose to everyday life and to that sweep of positive thought and passion which made possible the never-to-be-surpassed architectural miracles of the Middle Ages. If we ourselves could enter into that optimism we would perhaps be closer to their architecture.

The choir is the heart of a priory church and Christchurch Priory is the only monastic church in England in which the interior choir space (Plates 11 and 31) remains what it was before the Dissolution of the monasteries (*c*1538). Both the choir screen and the high altar reredos are in place, and are mostly intact from before the early sixteenth century. One of the misericord seats is thought to be the oldest in England (1210), and one is a portrait of Richard III.

Several unusual design elements distinguish the Priory: three widely separated Saxo-Norman crypts; the detail of the compound piers of the Norman nave (Plate 44); the large north porch; and the several transitional styles, between Norman Romanesque and Early English Gothic, between Early English and Decorated, and (at the chantries) between Perpendicular Gothic and Renaissance.

The interior spaces of the Priory are large and were designed, as with the great cathedrals, in the grand manner (Plates 11,31,44), but the exterior of the building as a whole is subject to much criticism (Plate 1).

The building has more than its share of unexplained parts where continuity appears to have been ignored or lost, and it is these major inconsistencies that constitute a challenge to the archaeological historian as much as to the architect today. The occasional break comes most often from the thirteenth century (Plate 35) rather than, as might be assumed, the nineteenth century.

Apparently, there was almost continuous building for some four hundred years. The Priory received generous gifts. Perhaps each new spurt of building activity was not always carefully thought through before the next was taken up. Perhaps funds were really too plentiful to require the most careful procedures.

This study is specifically based on what is evident today at the site. Architectural conclusions are frequently to be drawn from archaeological chaos; however, conclusions by documents will probably never be available because of the several possible answers to the puzzles of this building.

On this occasion, the purpose of the research undertaken over a decade has simply been to solve the puzzle of Christchurch Priory to the best of our ability in the late twentieth century. It is believed that the remarkable series of building changes and adaptations to the structure will also convey some new perceptions about the inherently flexible and pragmatic approach of the medieval master builders. This, in turn, can assist modern architectural thinking in a world of constant change, to see the historical perspectives where such adaptiveness has always been necessary in the fulfilment of requirements.

Plate 1

TEN CONCLUSIONS

There follows a synopsis of the ten specific conclusions I have drawn in several years of studying Christchurch Priory – conclusions that are best called informed speculations. As a package of three-dimensional ideas they do offer a coherent synthesis, freshly conceived to fit a broad chronology of circumstance and design. By placing them here together, before the lengthier discourse, clarity will be given to the substance of the article. See Plan, Sections and Plate 1. Such conclusions can fill many gaps in the sequence of construction. Such changes, after all, did happen – we can see it all before us – and so can be dealt with in this way, even though in some cases strict archaeological method cannot fully clarify what was achieved.

The Rib Vaults, North and South Transept Crypts

Initially, I shall touch on (and then put aside) a highly important question: the date of the rib vaults in the apses of the north and south transept crypts. The rib vault, of course, constitutes, along with the flying buttress, the central fact of Gothic architecture, and those of Durham Cathedral built in 1094 have been established as the earliest of all remaining examples in Europe. It is possible that these much smaller and much cruder rib vaults at Christchurch are earlier. (Dates given by Taylor Dyson in *The History of Christchurch Priory*, 1955, p82, allow for this.) A small crypt would have been an easy place in which to begin to experiment with a new and untried structural idea (Plates 2,3,8,9,10). The rib vaults at Christchurch may come to be dated quite a few years before those at Durham, and if this can be proved accurately it could change an important part of the history of Gothic architecture.

Plates 2 and 3

Measured plans, sections and elevations of the entire building have been published by Benjamin Ferrey in *A History of Christchurch Priory, Dorset*, 1841, and by GJ Coombs (with vertical dimensions) in the *Leeds and Yorkshire Architectural Society Proceedings* of 16 January 1908, and by others.

Conclusion 1: The weathermoulds above the choir ceiling vault at the east and west ends of the choir are evidence of the height of a former Early English choir.

Basis: At the west end they cross the lower windows of the east face of the Norman tower at the *middle* of the window. If they had been part of a Norman roof scheme they would not have conflicted with the windows in this flagrant manner.

Conclusion 2: The Early English choir in its principal phase was without aisles, although aisles were added later.

Basis: The weathermoulds, if extended downward toward the ground at the same steep slope, would have left no headroom for aisles.

Conclusion 3: There were two east transept apses at each transept arm, *inner* apses and *outer* apses. (The words *inner* and *outer* are used with respect to the central axis of the church.) (Other churches with aisleless choirs and with double, or implied double, transept apses facing east are Heilingenberg, Maria Laach, Würzburg, Old Sarum and Anglo-Norman Westminster. These were all earlier than Christchurch.)

Basis: The blocked opening of the second level inner apse north of the crossing can be seen from the interior of the transept. Also, segments of weathermould disappear into the Norman outer south transept apse – the apse that still exists today. The former roof was warped for drainage. Portions of weathermould can be seen on the east face of the east transept wall south of the crossing, both above the aisle roof (Plate 15) and below it. Also, we bear in mind that if the south arch into the choir aisle were symmetrically placed with

Plate 4

respect to the north arch, its north jamb would be about fifteen inches south of the existing north jamb. The existing south arch, of course, was totally rebuilt in the fifteenth or sixteenth centuries.

Conclusion 4: East of these apses, since there were no choir aisles, the steep choir roof would have been high enough to allow for ample light from high windows in the choir walls.
Basis: Note one window, high in the south transept. (This possibly indicates the height of the Early English choir windows.)

Conclusion 5: The nave was originally vaulted in stone, c1200.
Basis: The date of part of the existing nave roof is established at 1380. In the normal course of events there is need to replace oak timber seatings in about two hundred years. The original roof was built in the twelfth century. It is said that there was a fall of the crossing tower in the thirteenth century (Paul Cave, *The Romantic Story of Christchurch* and EC Mackensie and Walcott, *Memories of Christchurch Twynham*, 1868, p27). I believe this fall was on the nave and critically damaged the stone vault along with parts of the roof (Plate 38). Four or five feet of the lower ribs of this vault were noted by W Garbett who built the present wood vault c1820. (Plate 4; see later quote.)

Conclusion 6: There was also a *later* fall of the crossing tower, this time on the choir about the early or middle of the fifteenth century; the occasion then being taken to lower the choir floor to its present level. These two falls of the crossing tower are discussed later.

Conclusion 7: St Michael's Loft was built separately from and later than the Lady Chapel below it. It was not an integral part of the east end design, but is an addition ordered presumably by the Priory authorities for a still undetermined purpose. It most certainly spoils the exterior appearance of the otherwise fine building.
Basis: There appears from the ground to be no bonding of masonry between loft and choir, at least on the north side. (The loft extends

Plate 7

Plate 10

above all three bays of the existing Lady Chapel.) In addition, there is a shaving down of the Lady Chapel vault crown (seen under the loft floor) to accommodate gutters behind a parapet wall at that level (Plate 47).

There is major evidence in the different directions of facing of the stones in the transverse wall at the Jesse screen visible from the interior of the loft at its west end, says Garbett.

Conclusion 8: The ambulatory (this is the bay just east of the Jesse screen) was roofed originally at a low level.
Basis: There is a double transverse rib in the present high level Lady Chapel vault, low flying buttress tushes at this point and improvisations for loft access. Furthermore, there are eight inch offsets in the Lady Chapel walls above the stone vault at this point and adjustments for the seating of timbers. Just under the loft floor there are also putlog holes half covered by the stone vault of the Lady Chapel.

Conclusion 9: There was a, perhaps extensive, thirteenth century westwork.
Basis: There is a thirteenth (or late twelfth) century colonette projecting three inches above the triforium floor at its southwest bay. There are also blocked openings, with jambs and ribs, that lead into the fifteenth century tower at ground level from the west bay of the north aisle.

Conclusion 10: Walls, discovered from above by prodding, were found under the floor planks of the choir at the southeast of the stalls. They are Saxon or Norman supports for a higher and narrower central crypt, but they do not indicate a Norman choir narrower than the existing one. This would leave the wide east crossing opening without explanation.

The further examination of these ten *conclusions* is the substance of this article.

It is useful at this juncture now to list the major flaws seen in the

Plate 11

building today.

- The wall for the present vestry at its north side rises in plan to support at the middle of the vault span (Plate 23).
- There is a crudely improvised strut between the Montecute Chantries and the west bay of the north choir aisle (Plate 20).
- There is an approximately fifteen inch misalignment, in plan, and an over-sailing of the south parapets as they meet the crossing (Plate 16).
- There is drastic under-cutting of the east piers of the crossing to accommodate the choir screen (Plate 25).
- There is unresolved work in the buttressing of the west tower stairway on the north side of the tower (Plates 45 and 46).
- There are the confused cavity walls (largely inaccessible) at the south end of the south transept, having to do with access to a cross-over to the nave triforium at its high window, and also having to do with the transept gallery vault and with crypt access.
- The soffit of the east crossing arch is cracked, indicating a faulty rebuild of the tower (and of the thirteenth century choir after the later fall of the tower). This was no doubt the result of a decision to considerably raise the height of this arch to accommodate the thirteenth century choir. The soffit of the south crossing arch is spalled (Plate 18).

  At the west end of the choir, north of the crossing, there is visible under the floor boards the top of walls probably of the pre-Flambard crypt.

  Some minor excavation is needed to throw light on this and to explore for a pre-Flambard Saxo-Norman choir layout, if it exists. (See *conclusion 10.*)

- The addition of St Michael's Loft over the Lady Chapel is, of course, more than a 'flaw'. It is a major error of design judgement, presumably ordered by the Church authorities over the objection of the architect (Plate 1).

ABOVE: Plates 12 and 13; BELOW: Plates 14 and 15

Plates 18 and 19

Plate 20

CHOIR CRYPT

This is a unique (possibly Saxon) layout (Plates 5,6,49,50) of three crypts, one at the outer ends of each transept arm and one under the choir, each in its present form rebuilt by Norman builders. The east end of the choir crypt was again rebuilt in the late fifteenth century (perhaps also in the thirteenth century). It is possible that errors in the positioning of the three crypts account for an irregularity in the axis of the choir. This, in turn, would have a bearing on the narrowing of the fifteenth century choir aisles towards the west end each by about one foot.

The following prognosis is offered as regards the original choir floor level and the western limit of the original choir crypt.

- The crypt extended farther west than at present – probably all the way to the east crossing piers. (In its present form it would have been disproportionately short.)

- The level of the floor of the choir itself was about two feet higher than at present. In other words, it corresponded to the height of the top of the steps up from the aisles before the steps go down again to the present choir stalls. This accommodated below it a crypt height to match the Norman portion that exists today and placed it five or six feet higher than the aisles.

- The second and final fall of the crossing tower with consequent damage to the choir floor led to a lowering of the western bays of the choir floor and to the use of these bays for burials. These bays were sealed off by the present west wall of the crypt. The half-round on this wall at mid-point of the crypt may have supported an altar in the choir above.

At its east end the choir floor was raised in the late fifteenth

Plate 21

Plate 22

41

century and was made to support the heavy 'Jesse reredos' in its new position which is one bay farther east than it was originally. The floor of the Lady Chapel was discovered to have been sixteen inches lower than at present.

Although the inside span of the present choir is twenty-two feet, the inside span of the choir crypt north to south is about fourteen feet nine inches. It may be supposed that two stairways led down to the crypt at the west bay of the present choir, one on each side, from the inner face of the inner transept apses, each turning in at the bottom to the crypt (Plate 7). Photographs of an excavation about fifteen years ago by Mr Len Newman, construction clerk at the Priory for several decades, show some masonry work in these positions under the two west bays of the choir floor. However, the form of the work exposed remains unclear.

There are suggestive studies of various types of crypts that may relate to Christchurch.

- The *Victoria County History* (VCH) for Worcestershire describes the 1811 excavations at Evesham Abbey, and Mr Anthony Light has provided a translation of relevant medieval Latin, as edited in 1863.
- The *Royal Commission for Historical Monuments* (RCHM), Salisbury, vol 1, speculates very interestingly on the east end of Old Sarum.
- MF Hearn in 'Rectangular Ambulatories . . .' in the *Journal of the Society of Architectural Historians* (JSAH), 1971, also discusses these and other east end types.
- Wimborne Minster, studied in the RCHM, East Dorset, vol 5, 1975, is of great interest in analysing crypt arrangements and choir ends where, as at Christchurch, there is a considerable difference in floor level between aisles and choir.
- Ripon and Hexham crypts are widely and unsymmetrically separated. They are Saxon and very small.

Plate 25

Plate 26

CHOIR AND TRANSEPT IN NORMAN TIMES

It is suggested here that the Norman choir, as well as the early Early English choir, was without aisles and that there were full Norman galleries (as at Jumièges and the old Westminster) in both the north and south transepts. These were positioned about eighteen inches below the level of the floor above the nave aisles, and covered the full area of both transepts. It was not until 1150 that the church became a priory, therefore requiring a greater need for aisles at the choir.

There is strong evidence in favour of this aisleless choir in the north transept. Here, there is clearly to be seen a blocked opening that reaches up to well above the existing window over the present choir aisle (Plate 21). This opening would have intersected a roof over the choir aisle, had there been such an aisle. It gave access to an upper *inner* chapel, which would not have existed if it had not been built over a ground floor chapel below it. And this, of course, rules out the possibility of choir aisles, for the ground floor chapel would have accommodated a central altar. Its floor level was about six feet below the level of the choir floor immediately adjacent to it. The blocked opening is centred on the large Norman arch at ground floor level (Plate 24), which now does open into the north choir aisle and which originally opened into the ground floor inner chapel. The existence of a two-storeyed *outer* chapel is proven by another blocked opening centred directly over the north transept crypt. This opening is to be seen on both sides of the west wall of the 'tracing room', the room above the Montecute chapels.

The two-storeyed outer apse of the south transept still exists in almost its original form (Plate 32), but the inner chapel at the south may have had one storey only, at least in the earliest Norman phase.

The existing Norman window overhead, though partly rebuilt (Plate 26), argues against a second storey inner chapel at the south.

On the outer face of the east wall of the north transept above the roof are three corbels that supported the floor of the inner upper chapel on the north side, which has now vanished (Plate 21). Low, towards the floor of the 'tracing room' there is the top part of a pointed arch embedded in the east wall. These are difficult to interpret, but they could be thirteenth century stages toward what finally became the thirteenth century choir aisles. In addition, there is a large segmental relieving arch embedded in the exterior of the east wall of the north transept somewhat higher than the above described blocked opening to the upper inner chapel (Plate 21).

With regard to the form of the original Norman north transept chapels, the existing thirteenth century, so-called Montecute Chantries inevitably replaced the Norman forms. The northernmost part of these chantries centres on the crypt below. Immediately adjacent to the Norman stair tower is a short curved stretch of exterior wall (Plate 23), the arc of which has a radius too short to produce the expected apse – an example of which remains today at the south transept. It must be assumed from the necessities of geometry, therefore, that this arc merged into a flat Norman east wall – now having been replaced by late Early English work. There is also Early English work in the crypt below: the pointed arch of the centre bay of the crypt apse (Plate 10). The flat east wall of the Norman chapels must have extended south to the choir, for it would have included the two lower chapels. The inner one of these must have centred on the large existing Norman arch that now leads into the north choir aisle. In the 'tracing room' above the Montecute Chantries is also embedded a Norman jamb at the side of the thirteenth century east window.

The existing thirteenth century 'older Lady Chapel' (the present day vestry) crowds in onto the west bay of the existing fifteenth century south choir aisle, showing again that in some way the clergy of the thirteenth century were adapting an aisleless choir and the double transept chapels to provide an aisled choir. This fifteenth

Plate 27

century choir aisle wall angles in to the choir aisle at this point and it does not at all coincide geometrically with the correct positioning of support for the vestry ceiling vaults (Plate 23). In the case of the two very small westernmost bays of the vestry, the wall is perhaps four feet too far south, and in the case of the two easternmost bays it is perhaps one and a half feet too far south – in both cases it strikes the ceiling in the middle of the vault cells. The easternmost bays were built at a different time than those on the west, the ribs being differently moulded.

In plan, if we shift this choir aisle wall four feet to the north to what must have been its original position (correctly supporting the vestry ceiling vault) we find that there would be little space for a south choir aisle. There would, however, have been space for an inner apse (or inner chapel), and this would have centred on the original Norman arch that must have been symmetrically placed in relation to the existing Norman arch north of the crossing. The present arch into the choir aisle at the south of the crossing was built in the late fifteenth century. What is now the vestry was built, as noted, in two stages and crowded between these two Norman chapels. Above it (visible from the transept) are the remains of what appears to be a window jamb shaft hidden in the plaster. Possibly, it is of Norman design; the opening blocked by the early sixteenth century builders. It might, therefore, confirm that the inner apse (or chapel) was only one storey which, in turn, coordinates with the location of the exterior weathermould at this point (Plate 15).

It should be said that the existing semicircular outer apse on the south centres on the crypt below. In this south crypt at the east end is an opening, now blocked (Plate 8). To where did it lead? To the conventual buildings, to the crypt of the choir, or to a burial ground? Perhaps both transept crypts were used as burial crypts or as charnel houses at one time. The south transept crypt retains spots of its original painted Norman decoration.

The rib vaults of the crypt apses (Plates 2,3,8,9,10) may eventually be dated (with respect to McGee's findings in 'Early Vaults of St Etiènne of Beauvais' in the *Journal of the Society of Architectural*

Plate 30

51

Historians, March 1986) to the 1070s – placing them much earlier than those of Durham, hitherto held to be the oldest. Flambard is said to have received the patronage of Christchurch in 1093 – though even this is difficult to confirm. Some excavation to search for Saxon work in the crypts would assist. And an even more thorough search of documents, than scholars have yet made, would be useful. (Also, see CH Moore, *The Medieval Church Architecture of England*, Macmillan, 1912, pp15-20 for an excellent analysis, but, I believe, an incorrect dating).

Regarding the two transept roofs (Plate 16), examination of the masonry on the south face of the wall above the south crossing arch and under the very old transept roof timbers, shows the original crossing tower construction against which the south transept roof abutted. When the nave roof was continued over the crossing, after the demise of the tower, it was necessary to jog the nave parapets up and down in order to match the new levels, and there is as much as a fifteen inch non-alignment in plan (Plate 16). The corners of the tower slightly project in plan beyond the four abutting wings. It is possible to assume that the form and height of the north transept roof was the same as that at the south.

The sixteenth century builders constructed an additional south transept wall at ground level three or four feet *inside* the already existing south wall, presumably to support access to the south nave aisle gallery – for the transept galleries that served this function were being removed. This additional wall seriously cramps the outer lower chapel entrance.

It should be noted that the famous northeast stair tower (Plate 22) at the north transept was higher than it is now, and that the present clumsy re-capping (an awkward geometrical problem admittedly) was no doubt Victorian.

Ironically, the difficult geometry for the vaulting of irregular Montecute Chantries resulted in a totally successful late thirteenth century whimsy that is one of the Priory's special glories (Plate 27).

CONTINUED DEVELOPMENT OF NORMAN AND THIRTEENTH CENTURY EAST END CONFIGURATION

I have assumed that, as was customary, the Norman building terminated in an apsidal choir. The height of the Norman choir roof timbers and tie-beams can be closely determined if a transverse vertical section through the choir is envisioned looking west toward the east arch of the crossing. Above the east crossing arch and seen from under the crossing by looking toward the east are four round-headed windows in what was the east wall of the Norman crossing tower. The east arch of the crossing which supported the tower was much lower than it is today. (This hypothetical section would also include the east faces of the two transept arms with inner and outer, upper and lower chapels.)

The Norman choir roof would have been designed to abut the central tower *below* these four windows so to allow daylight to enter the crossing – daylight being a pressing need in cruciform churches. The roof would rise as high as possible, but within that limit. The semicircular terminal apse of the choir itself would have been designed in the usual way to equal or exceed the height of the existing south transept apse. On a section-elevation, these considerations would determine the height of the choir roof timbers and tie-beams with respect to the Norman east crossing arch. We can assume that the roof timber seating and tie-beam scheme of Norman Winchester would have been comparable to that of the Norman Priory at Christchurch. (For this Winchester scheme see Francis Bond's *An Introduction to English Church Architecture*, 1913, p796.) And this height is confirmed by the, previously noted, single (somewhat remodelled) Norman window (Plate 26) high in the east wall of the south transept above the choir aisle. This window probably establishes the height of the upper storey of a two-storey

Plate 31

Plate 32

Norman choir. It cannot be known if the successive choirs were vaulted in stone, although at the east end of the south choir aisle before the existing vault and under the roof structure there does seem to be evidence of some early buttresses. Of greatest interest in all of this (see *conclusion 1*) is the well preserved weathermould on the east face of the crossing arch which, as noted, can only be examined by going above the stone vault of the present choir. This weathermould at the west end of the choir angles sharply across the mid-point of the lower outer pair of windows, passing continuously across them (Plates 12 and 19). These lower windows are now walled-up flush with the west edge of their jambs. The weathermould 'nicks' a small lower corner of the upper inner pair of windows, which today still admit light to the crossing (Plate 17). We note that the arris of the jambs of the two outer lower windows is squared, while that of the upper inner windows is rounded. Were these four windows in the east wall of the Norman crossing tower placed at different times?

Here is found another puzzle: there is what seems to be a hinge pivot of uncorroded metal built into the south jamb of the north lower window, and a rebate is cut in the stone surrounds of both lower windows and in the weathermould itself, which might have allowed a shutter to open out, away from the tower (Plate 13). There may have been a gallery at lantern level (the wall is thick and has been worked in offsets) later filled in for added strength (Plates 18 and 19). Yet the shutter, if there was one, would not have been workable because its diagonal lower edge would, of course, not be able to open against the slope of the choir roof. How, therefore, does one explain this 'hinge pivot'? Perhaps there was a manually placed shutter, not hinged, but barred. This remains unsolved.

The location of the east end of the Norman choir cannot easily be determined. The east bay of the crypt was rebuilt after Norman times and was strengthened to bear the weight of the 'Jesse reredos' in its present position. And in these changes, along with the complete rebuild of the choir to its present splendid late Gothic design (late fifteenth and early sixteenth centuries), the thirteenth century choir structure has been lost, except for what was the east parapet wall of the choir over the 'Jesse reredos' (Plate 16), and the east (Plate 14) and west (Plate 7) weathermoulds, as discussed.

In all of this we conclude that there were two early and perhaps unfinished choirs, one pre-Flambard and one under Flambard; and also the Early English choirs developing form over the decades, and at first without aisles.

Plates 35 and 36

NAVE VAULT AND
TWO TOWER FALLS

The confused traditions of the two different tower falls and the inferences produced by Garbett below (quoted in Ferrey, 1841) lead me to propose that there were just two falls of the tower and/or spire. Did it fall on the nave, the transepts or the choir? And when? The *Victoria County History* states: 'It is said to have fallen in the fifteenth century.'

In considering the probably fourteenth century timber roof still in place over his plaster nave ceiling Garbett has this to say:

> ... *if we institute a fair comparison of the durability of timber roofing, we shall find good reason to conclude that the lapse of two hundred or at the most two hundred and fifty years would not have rendered the renewal of the roof* (Plates 28,29,38) *of such a building necessary if an accident had not happened to destroy it; secondly that the present roof is composed principally of timbers which formed the roof corresponding with the slope of the gable wall now rising above it, the roof being reconstructed with the addition of tie-beams in consequence of the decay of the members connected with the walls and gutters; and thirdly we may refer to the moulded stone ribs which, before the construction of the present ceiling in the year 1819, were seen rising to the height of four or five feet from the capitals of the columns in the nave ... I much incline to the opinion that towards the end of the twelfth century, or perhaps somewhat after, the nave was vaulted with stone, and that the central tower begun by Flambard was continued and surmounted by a spire (probably not of stone) which either through some casualty of tempest or weakness of structure, fell upon the roof and*

Plate 39

Plate 40

destroyed or so much injured the vaulted ceiling as to render its removal necessary[1]. After this calamity I visualize the shattered walls of the central tower were reduced in three sides to the height we now find them and that the east side was rebuilt to form the gable end of the new roof …

If Garbett is correct (and I believe he is), there was a nave vaulted in stone by the end of the twelfth century. The small stone corbels now projecting from north and south clerestory walls above the nave ceiling were for the tie-beams. CH Moore, *Medieval Church Architecture of England*, Macmillan, 1912, states, regarding Christchurch, that 'flying buttresses formerly sprung in the nave triforium'. However that may be, the vaulting of the nave aisles at this time brought added support to the nave vault. The Christchurch nave has a clear span of twenty-seven feet. As at St Etiènne of Beauvais (McGee), an extensive set of buttresses need not be expected. For comparison, the Durham nave was vaulted by 1133 and has a clear span of about thirty-eight feet.

The existing very early Early English clerestory was built to receive the nave vault. A little later, the aisles were revaulted in that style.

A *later* fall of the rebuilt central tower damaging the choir floor at its west end and not damaging the 'Jesse reredos' is, as noted, postulated to have been the occasion for the lowering of the floor of this part of the choir. Also to be noticed is the spalled soffit of the south crossing arch, indicating structural over-stressing (Plate 18). The fault in the soffit of the east crossing arch is, as noted, very evident, the east arch having been raised from its original Norman height to accommodate a thirteenth century choir.

It is evident that the double pier shafts of the nave arcade do not extend to the top of the nave wall, as they would have done if they had supported a wood roof. They are cut short for the support of vault corbelling (Plate 44).

We should like to have Garbett's explanation of the gable trace of a presumed original higher roof slope on the east face of the west tower. The decay in the tie-beams and the fitting to a lower roof slope (the present slope) must have taken place after the west tower was built. This trace has been filled with mortar and must therefore have been for a lead flashing. Are the west tower date, the timber date and the more frequent later use of lead compatible?

The two east crossing piers were very deeply undercut when the choir screen was installed. The result is disorderly (Plate 25). The provenance of that elaborate and heavy screen remains another Christchurch mystery. Ferrey suggests it was taken from another abbey at the time of the Dissolution. It is, at least partly, in the Decorated style.

[1]Pevsner speaks of the Norman clerestory not surviving, though he avoids the vault question.

Plates 41 and 42

Plates 43 and 44

ORIGINAL CHURCH AT THE WEST END

Along with the crypts and transepts, the four central crossing piers constitute the earliest remaining Norman work at Christchurch, and the piers are thought to have been completed *c*1120.

Next, the nave, a very fine Norman structure, was built (Plate 44). The prominent design theme is heavy double half-round pier shafts and soffit mouldings expressed consistently in the compound piers and arcades. The nave was constructed by Ranulf Flambard who, at the same time, was working on Durham Cathedral. Christchurch nave was probably completed before 1150. The fine north porch (revaulted in Victorian times) is thirteenth century. Also thirteenth century is the somewhat earlier revaulting of the south and north nave aisles and the refacing of the outside of the north nave aisle wall below the Norman gallery windows, along with the elegantly re-done north aisle window recesses and tracery. The clerestory represents very early Early English work – in the same style as the rest.

The existing west front with its fine fifteenth century west tower and westernmost aisle bays have obliterated or confused almost all trace of the Norman westwork, and we must reason by supposition as we look back to Norman days (Plate 46). The existing west front of the Augustinian Norman priory of Jedburgh in Scotland, though probably built slightly after Christchurch, offers a partial design parallel. At Christchurch the Norman west front stood at the east face of the present fifteenth century west tower, and evidence has been recorded of a blocked circular stair set in what is now the northeast corner of the tower at ground level. (See KF Wiltshire's thorough-going research thesis, *Christchurch Priory*, 1958.)

In the south wall of the south nave aisle just west of the

eighteenth century southwest door recent discoveries have been described by John R Forster in his wide-ranging *Christchurch Priory*, 1985:

> *On the south side of the aisle close to the upper part of the chapel Memorial screen can be seen a short length of arch moulding terminating in a carved female head ... The removal of rubble (behind this wall) revealed the stone infilling of the arch, and lastly the lower part of a circular wall, probably part of the Norman turret in which the aisle would have terminated.*

The turret probably contained a stair that led to conventual buildings – the monks' dorter was thought to be adjacent across the slype. But it must be admitted that it is difficult to make out the stair within the heaped rubble in the turret. There are also the remains of a strong relieving arch in the south wall under the short length of arch moulding, noted above. These may have been part of the west front work. Opposite on the north, immediately west of the north porch entrance door is the thirteenth century stair, which is used today for access to the space over the north porch, the north triforium and bell-tower. There was no Norman north door at this corner of the building.

It is difficult to interpret the Conventual Seal (Plate 42). Are the outer turrets on this Seal to be found at the plane of the west front or at the plane of the transepts? If the Seal does have representational meaning, I believe the latter to be the case, thus reinforcing a supposition of the Jedburgh scheme. There, the high rose window is a fifteenth century addition. (The speculative perspective drawing of the Christchurch west front made in the 1950s by AE Henderson is interesting, but I think not plausible.) There is the indication, previously noted at the south clerestory level, of an interior wall passage that would have run straight across the west front connecting the clerestories. If this is correct it would have necessitated a slightly lower west window than at Jedburgh. This is all that can be postulated of the Norman work at the west end.

The west bays of both north and south nave aisles contain

Plates 45 and 46

especially important evidence of the thirteenth century rebuild of much of Christchurch Priory – of which so little remains today (Plate 46). The west tower is fifteenth century. But what was where it now stands? Once more, along with Garbett, I believe the thirteenth century work included a west porch.

At the time of the building of the present tower, provision was made for vaulting the end bays of both aisles and at a somewhat higher level than the aisles themselves. In these end bays are wall ribs and corner springers, some of which are left uncarved. In the south bay there is part of a stone ceiling vault cell left in place. All of this is from the fifteenth century.

Evidence of the thirteenth century is also clear. There are 'thirteenth century' shafts and capitals at what are now the two east piers of the west tower, and from these capitals toward the west spring amputated wall arches in high relief on the blocked-in wall. These occur below the fifteenth century wall ribs and are embedded in the fifteenth century wall work (Plate 45).

Furthermore, at about three feet above triforium level on the south there is a thirteenth century colonette capital on a shaft that rises at the existing tower pier from the triforium floor (Plate 41). A length of an embedded thirteenth century arch and carved corbel in the south wall of the south bay at ground level has already been noted.

There are heavy north and south thrusting structural buttresses at the east face of the tower (Plate 45), and there is a heavy buttress against the west face of the stair that leads up to the thirteenth century space over the north porch.

There is further evidence of a thirteenth century west porch which is scattered, partial and unresolved so as to make an intelligible written discussion of it impossible. Pevsner says he is open to a 'westwork' solution to the problem – though he would date it Norman. Why? A 'westwork' is a deep or porch-like treatment.

Possible west porch parallels might be examined to shed light on all this, such as at:

Melrose Abbey, Scotland

Snettisham, Norfolk

Fountains, Rievaulx and Byland Abbeys, Yorkshire

St Nicolas, Caen

Tournus and Fleury Abbeys, Burgundy

Pontigny Abbey, Burgundy

Strata Florida Abbey, Cardigan

But, because of the very slender evidence at Christchurch, perhaps nothing definite on the form of the thirteenth century west front can be concluded. There are, however, said to have been excavations for another purpose in this area. The author has not located these.

Plates 47 and 48

Plates 49 and 50

THE EXISTING EAST ARM OF CHRISTCHURCH

I quote again, with agreement, Garbett who we saw was the architect of the plaster nave ceiling 'vault' of 1820 and who, in turn, was quoted by Benjamin Ferrey (also a Christchurch Priory architect) in his *Antiquities of the Priory of Christchurch*, published 1841:

> *The Lady-chapel (with north and south bays now forming the continuation of the choir aisles) was unquestionably built previous to the erection of the present choir and its aisles. This is rendered evident not only by the butt of the masonry, but by the window, or rather doorway, discoverable in what was the west wall of the Lady-chapel in a situation now between the vaulted ceiling of that edifice and the floor of St Michael's Loft as shown in the longitudinal section. It is further evident that the present choir must have been erected previous to St Michael's Loft, inasmuch as it is found that the heightening of the height of the wall last mentioned formed, upon the rebuilding of the choir, the eastern wall of that part of the church, in which wall another window or doorway is found between the stone vaulted ceiling of the choir and the roof at the place seen in the same section. Now to connect this theory of the progress of the structure we must observe that the facing of the part of the wall first mentioned[1] is towards the west, and that the second part is towards the east, forming an outward face before the addition of the additional storey was raised upon the Lady-chapel to be dedicated to St Michael.*

After examination at the site I believe Garbett is correct with regard to the east facing. The exceptionally fine Perpendicular Lady Chapel can be dated definitely by tombs to a design made *c*1400.

I propose that there was still an earlier construction phase that produced initially only the two east bays of the Lady Chapel vaulted as they stand today, but with an ambulatory bay whose ceiling was at the lower level of the present choir aisle vault – the same low level as the east bays and chapels of the aisles that were built and bonded with the Lady Chapel. This scheme would have been a normal one, whereas the present high ambulatory bay is unusual. It would then follow that this low ambulatory bay of the Lady Chapel was raised to its present height in order that the large St Michael's Loft could be placed on three bays instead of only two, and that both these changes occurred after the choir and choir aisles were built.

Further evidence for this is the double transverse ceiling rib with its double corbels that separates the ambulatory and the Lady Chapel proper (Plate 43). There is also a slightly different sculptural treatment of the west faces of these corbels. They may be taken from different stone quarries. (Militating against this proposal is the fact that the double rib might be explained by the geometry required in passing the continuously high vault around a heavy pier at this point.)

So when Dr John Harvey in *The Perpendicular Style,* Batsford, 1978, touches on the 'rather enigmatic Lady Chapel at Christchurch' this high ambulatory bay becomes part of the 'enigma'.

There are further points that reinforce my *conclusions 1 and 8.*

The stairs to St Michael's Loft on both north (Plates 33 and 34) and south are crowded awkwardly, and at a later date, between the earlier east chapels' buttresses. Above the chapels' roofs it can be seen that the higher and inner flights of the stair towers were corbelled out on insets after the Lady Chapel wall had been built (Plate 39).

The existing tushes for low flying buttresses at this point (Plate 39), that is at the Lady Chapel ambulatory, demonstrate the builders' indecisions.

- Were these flying buttresses, north and south, used to bolster a low level ambulatory vault? I believe they were.
- Was this to substitute for the heavy stepped buttress scheme for the two east Lady Chapel bays, since, because of the east

aisle chapels, there was no room for these in plan?

When the loft (with its extensive stair towers access) was built over the full three bays it made buttresses unnecessary and the low flying buttresses were dismantled.

– Was there uncertainty about the need for any buttress at all, because of the existence of the east aisle chapels alone, and was loft access gained for a time by wood stairs only?

There are through vertical mortar joints in the outer aisle walls at positions just west of the 'Jesse reredos', the western choir aisles having been built, as noted, after the Lady Chapel with the east aisle and chapel bays.

JHP Gibb's reconstruction research at the east end of Sherborne Abbey illustrates in general terms a related roof scheme.

The decision to add the loft above the Lady Chapel was an altogether unfortunate one aesthetically and could hardly have been part of the thinking of the architect of the elegant Lady Chapel itself. And then, the unfinished and unresolved parapet (Plate 40). Perhaps the Dissolution came before it could be finished off.

Possibly, there were changes of plan that lead to otherwise inexplicable stops and starts. And possibly there were occasional errors in the work. The Priory was said to have been a wealthy one. The changes and additions may, for this very reason, have been ordered rather recklessly by non-designers. How should we interpret the unnecessarily heavy east Lady Chapel buttresses?

The easternmost bay of the Norman choir crypt was remodelled or extended eastward and strengthened to take the 'Jesse reredos' in its new and present location. Only archaeological excavation could establish the exact termination of the Norman choir. Did the choir have three bays east of the crossing or four as at present?

We have noticed when discussing the four Norman windows in the east face of the crossing tower that there was a thirteenth century rebuild of the choir and that the inner transept chapels north and south of the crossing would have been incompatible with an aisled Norman choir. So were there choir aisles in the thirteenth century structure? I think there eventually were. There were probably time overlaps in the various building programmes, and also transitions – certain parts having been begun before what they depended on had been completed. Ecclesiastical requirements were changing and expanding in the twelfth and thirteenth centuries, and at the same time the priories and monasteries prospered.

A prime example of these overlaps would involve, as previously discussed, the four windows in the east wall of the central crossing over the east crossing arch. The two lower windows could have been built concurrently with the progress of the Norman choir (never completed). The two upper windows and the weathermould would have been concurrent with the Montecute Chapels, say $c1260$, and with the vestry. It may have been at this time that the two lower windows were blocked and the weathermould built.

From tombs and initials in the existing building, both the Lady Chapel and choir have been dated, as noted, $c1400$ and $c1500$, respectively. The loft followed on after the choir and just before the Dissolution.

[1]*The author does not at all confirm the west facing masonry. At this point, either Garbett or Ferrey is confused.*

APPENDIX A

It will help further research to list several matters that have not been dealt with at all in this monograph. They each may have important ramifications.

- The nave triforium buttresses and 'thirteenth century' arches are visible from within the triforiums over the arcades.
- The evidence of choir buttresses can be seen from between the south choir aisle roof and the choir aisle vault, toward the east.
- The 'prop' supporting the 'tracing room' over the Montecute chantry.
- The large newel in the stair of the northeast transept tower.
- Location of original access to the central crypt.
- Measured vertical elevations, as described above, of both sides of the east wall of both transepts with crossing arch, the upper wall setbacks, the four windows and the weathermould.
- Possible exterior entrances to the three crypts.
- There are, as noted, photographs, with their location key, of walls or footings underneath the choir floor planks. (See Mr Len Newman, mason for the Priory for many years.)
- Search for through vertical junctions in masonry where appropriate, and especially for horizontal build stops in the west wall of the loft at floor level.
- Berkeley chapel and vestry squints.
- Support for the southwest flying buttress of the choir.
- Vestry wall thicknesses.
- Liturgical needs and changes over the centuries.
- Offsets in Lady Chapel walls over the vault, as noted.
- Evidence for a lower Lady Chapel floor, and its relation to the central crypt.
- 'Construction door' in the east wall of the Lady Chapel.
- Interpretations (and reliability) of the various Seals.
- The style of the present west tower in the overall context of the Somerset towers.
- Torregiano and the Salisbury Chantry and other traces of the Renaissance style.

APPENDIX B

It is interesting to realise that in the Romanesque and medieval centuries there was an internationalism that does not exist today. The Channel was not a barrier; architectural influences travelled easily and sometimes quickly. There follows a short list, no doubt incomplete, of pre-Christchurch structures conceivably influential in the Priory transept apse layout.

Heiligenberg St Michael

Metz Cathedral

Limbourg-on-the-Hardt

Pre-Conquest Westminster

Goslar

There follows a further list, not demonstrably earlier than the Priory but showing parallels in some respect.

Jedburgh, Scotland	Lessay
Wimborne Minster	Domfront
Bernay	St George Boscherville
Southwell	Sherborne (before the fire)
Romsey	Jumièges
Roche	Ursel
Blyth	Paray-le-Monial
Melbourne	Sannezzaro Sesia
New Shoreham	St Etiènne, Beauvais
Evesham	St Michele, Pavia
St Vincent, Soignies	Helmstadt
St Bavo of Ghent	… and several typical Cistercian Abbeys, such as Strata Florida, Cardigan

APPENDIX C

As stated, there is no thoroughly definitive research on any of the ten speculations enumerated in the synopsis of this article. There is, however, partial and piecemeal opinion and some tangential viewpoints. It would be impossible to equate each of the scholars listed below with particular subject matter, but all have interested themselves with aspects of Christchurch Priory archaeology. It is with apologies that I append this list of scholars, but it does indicate a pervasive interest in Christchurch.

Bony	Moore, CM (with drawings)
Grodecki	Wiltshire (with drawings)
Fernie	Clapham
Hearn	Porter
Harvey	Lethaby
Ferrey (with drawings)	Sharpe
Henderson, AE (with drawings)	Gibb
Coombs (with drawings)	Dyson
Peers	McGee
Pevsner	Walcott
Batsford	Jones, PT
Braun	Cook, GH
Addison	Druit, H (with drawings)

PLAN AND SECTIONS

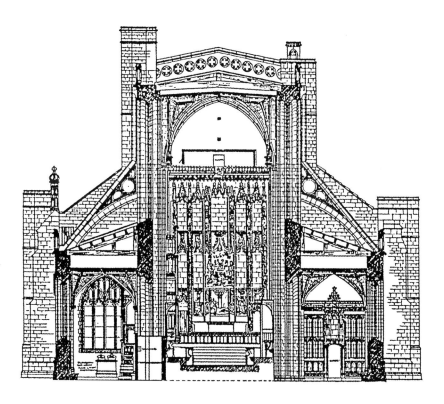

Cross-section through Choir

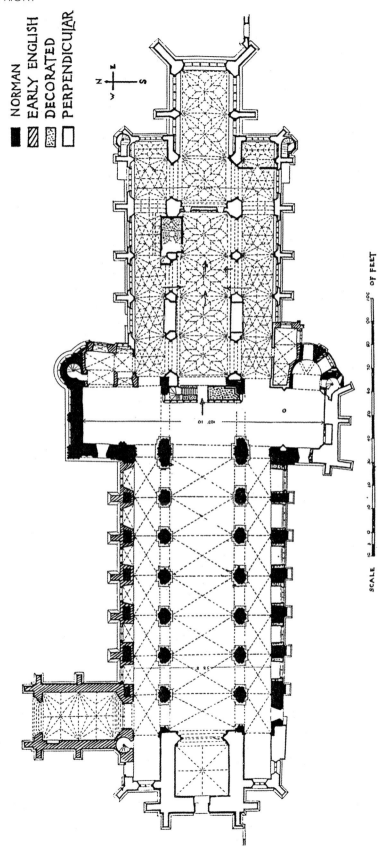

NORMAN
EARLY ENGLISH
DECORATED
PERPENDICULAR

SCALE   OF FEET

Plan of Christchurch Priory

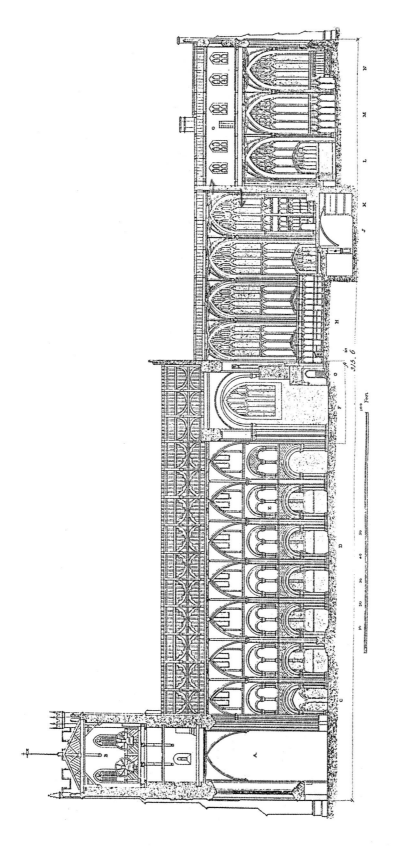

Longitudinal section

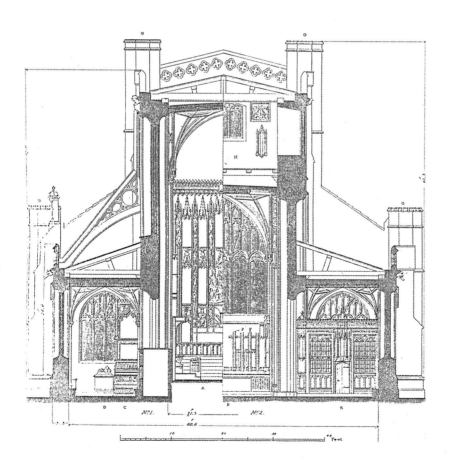

Half-section through the Choir and the Lady Chapel

Transverse-section of the Nave

PRINCIPAL DIMENSIONS OF THE PRIORY CHURCH

	Feet	Inches	Metres
Length, from western entrance of the tower to eastern extremity of Lady Chapel	311	4	94.88
Length of nave	118	9	36.19
Mean breadth of nave (the western extremity is somewhat wider than the eastern end)	27	9	8.46
Breadth of nave with aisles	58	5	17.80
Extreme height of nave vaulting	58	0	17.68
Mean circumference of large columns	36	6	11.12
Length of nave aisles	139	11	42.65
Breadth of nave aisles (excluding 4ft space between the great columns)	10	10	3.30
Length of transept	101	2	30.84
Mean breadth of transept	24	4	7.42
Thickness of entrance screen to great choir	6	10	2.08
Length of great choir from entrance screen to Jesse screen	70	0	21.33
Breadth of choir	21	3	6.48
Breadth between the stalls	11	5	3.48
Height of choir vaulting	60	0	18.29
Breadth of choir with aisles	60	6	18.44
Length of choir aisles	109	5	33.35
Breadth of ambulatory	21	2	6.45
Length of Lady Chapel	36	4	11.07
Breadth of Lady Chapel	21	1	6.42
Interior length of north porch	35	6	10.82
Breadth of north porch	19	7	5.97
Height of tower	120	0	36.57
Number of steps to the top 189			
Length of tower, from entrance to nave	27	9	8.46
Breadth of tower	22	4	.6.80
Length of the salmon weather vane on central flagstaff	5	4	1.62
Weight of salmon 30lbs (13.61kg)			
Height of fish above top of tower (it was put into position in 1969 by voluntary labour)	32	0	9.75
Length of St Michael's Loft (the museum over the Lady Chapel)	58	3	17.75
Breadth of St Michael's Loft	23	4	7.11
The gist, or boundary line, of the whole building following angles made by buttresses and other projections	1304	0	397.44

LIST OF PLATES

were in transition and the building programmes were to a large extent continuous.

15   Continuation of weathermould toward the south, striking the two-storey south transept apse. This indicates a single storey structure at this point. (See Plate 26.)

16   View of roofs east from west tower shows matters of great interest.
      – Misalignment of Lady Chapel and loft.
      – Upper and lower stairs to loft.
      – Gable formed after the first fall of the central tower toward the nave and the reconstruction of the nave (and crossing) roof at its present lower pitch.
      – The original north transept roof is also assumed to have abutted the central tower as did the south transept roof seen here.
      – The oversail of the south parapet can be seen at this point.
      – On the west face of the north transept can be seen the removal of a decorative cluster of colonette shafts.

17   Crest of this same thirteenth century weathermould in east face of Norman crossing between the two upper inner windows. The non-aligned jointing between the weathermould and the tower itself demonstrates that the mould was set into the tower after the latter was built.

18   View toward the choir from under the spalled south crossing arch and through the cracked east crossing arch. Here is seen lower and upper Norman windows with the varying wall thicknesses that indicate efforts to strengthen the tower base after the two falls.

19   Interior of crossing showing the four early windows in east crossing arch.

20   Improvised 'prop' to reinforce oversail of the 'tracing room' at the north choir aisle. View looks into the thirteenth century Montecute Chantries. (See Plate 21.) Even after careful examination the aisle roof space south of this prop does not establish the forms of these Norman inner apses, upper and lower.

21   Oversail of the so-called 'tracing room' above the Montecute Chantries at the east face of the north transept, made necessary when choir aisles were added. South of the oversail and adjacent to it is seen the blocking of the opening for the Norman inner upper apse, in the middle of which is now a thirteenth century window. Below this window can be seen the three projecting corbels that supported the wood floor of the apse, and above the blocking can be seen the relieving arch that spanned the opening to the apse. (See *conclusions 2 and 3*.)

22   Norman northeast transept tower showing modified roof. The well known Norman northeast transept tower. Adjacent to the tower wall is a section of the curved wall leading into the flat Norman apses that originally extended in two-storey form across to the wall of the choir. At that time there was, of course, no 'oversail' because there were no obstructing choir aisles.

23   Thirteenth century vaults of the 'vestry' with a wall of the south choir aisle, looking northwest. Note: the wall was built *after* the vaults. Vault ribs show a difference of moulding styles. The inner apse south of the crossing was of only one storey. (See Plate 15.)

24   Interior face of north transept. On the right at ground level is the original Norman opening into the inner lower apse, and above it is the blocked opening of the inner upper apse. (See Plate 21.) On the left at ground level are the present thirteenth century Montecute Chantries in space formerly used by Norman outer apses. Farther to the north (out of view to the left) at the upper level is the now blocked large arch opening to the original outer Norman apse.

25   Northeast crossing pier (with early Norman capital) showing the blocked inner upper apse opening and the very severe under-cutting of east piers (north and also south) to accommodate the Gothic choir screen, which was undoubtedly brought from another location.

26   This view toward the crossing from the southeast shows how skilful working out of interior spaces over the centuries can result in awkward, unresolved exteriors. What is the support for the small abutment that receives the thrust (if any) of the western most flying buttress of the choir? This abutment occurs in plan above a transverse rib of the present vestry which would not meet the structural need, and since a structural solution is impossible in this unexpected corner, the matter went by default and the flying buttress was put in by habit.

27   Whimsical vault at awkward Montecute Chantries at east face of north transept.

28/29 Carved and painted relief ornaments on angle braces of the nave roof, for viewing from the floor, after stone vault was destroyed by the first fall of the central tower. The relief ornament can be dated after 1330, says Peers in the *Victoria County History*. Plate 28, a carpenter's self-portrait?

30   Northwest pier of crossing looking toward nave.

31   Choir vault, looking west. This vault is later than, but very similar to, the Lady Chapel vault.

32   The Norman south transept apse, also showing the south transept roof

and at lower right the present day 'vestry', thirteenth century. (See Plates 15,23,26.)

33   Improvisations north of the two western bays of the Lady Chapel showing loft access from outside, as provided in the early sixteenth century, penetrating the slightly earlier heavy stepped buttress. The situation on the south side, low flying buttress and all, was closely parallel. The exterior entrance is now blocked and a door to the loft is cut from inside the building.

34   North stair access to loft.

35   An anomaly of the changing times. One pilaster of the north wall of the nave in the north aisle breaks abruptly from the governing Norman nave arcade motif to the transitional style of the aisle vault. Just seen at the right is a jamb of the still later Early English vaulted window recess. These unresolved junctures are common at Christchurch. They may be, paradoxically, the result of too much speed and too much money. The Priory was a wealthy one.

36   Thirteenth century window alcove at Norman south transept apse.

37   Northwest pier of crossing seen from the northeast, showing many revised ideas.

38   Timber roof framing over nave.

39   The low level flying buttress tush and the oversail of the upper stair tower to the loft – both at the south side of the Lady Chapel. Again, these demonstrate the builders' puzzlement in handling changing needs. The text explains these complex enigmas at some length. (See Plate 40.)

40   South side of the choir, Lady Chapel and St Michael's Loft, looking east. At the base of the inner loft stair tower can be seen the tushes of the low level flying buttress of Plate 39. The missing parapet over the choir is all too evident in this view, as is the visually disconcerting loft.

41   Thirteenth century colonettes of the Priory westwork before the construction of the fifteenth century west tower. The colonettes are seen in the south nave triforium behind the southeast corner of the tower. But the form of the vanished westwork is not revealed (See *conclusion 9.*)

42   Conventual Seal.

43   The double transverse ceiling vault rib separating the ambulatory and the Lady Chapel. (See the discussions and *conclusions 7 and 8.*)

44   North nave arcade, triforium and clerestory. See the pervasive Norman

Christchurch motif – the double half-round.

45 Half arch buttress against the northeast corner of the fifteenth century west tower. Notice the abrupt changes of scheme regarding the blocked opening for westwork in the space appropriated by the west tower. (See *conclusion 9*.) Just above and adjacent to this area is a concentration of minor mysteries, the meanings of which cannot be conveyed except during examination at the site.

46 North face of northeast pier of tower, seen from westernmost aisle bay.

47 Top of the Lady Chapel vault showing the shaving of excess masonry to make room for a roof gutter. (See *conclusion 7* for the discussion of this evidence.) The loft was an afterthought; not in the elegant Lady Chapel design.

48 Present day stone mason's maintenance tools.

49/50 This is no doubt Saxon work. It was discovered in detritus in the ruins of the southwest stair tower at the south aisle of the nave, but that location is probably incidental. It is surely a part of a baptismal font.

BIBLIOGRAPHY

B Ferrey, *Antiquities of the Priory at Christchurch*, 1841.

B Ferrey, *A History of Christchurch Priory, Dorset*, 1841.

EC MacKensie and Walcott, *Memories of Christchurch, Twynham*, 1868.

GJ Coombs, *Leeds and Yorkshire Architectural Society Proceedings*, 16 January, 1908.

CH Moore, *The Medieval Church Architecture of England*, Macmillan, 1912.

F Bond, *An Introduction to English Church Architecture*, 1913.

H Batsford and C Fry, *The Greater English Church*, Batsford, London, 1940.

T Dyson, *The History of Christchurch Priory*, 1955.

KF Wiltshire, *Christchurch Priory*, 1958.

J Betjeman (Ed), *Collins Guide to English Parish Churches*, Collins, London, 1958.

N Pevsner, 'The Early and Classic Gothic Style/ The Late Gothic Style' in *An Outline of European Architecture* (Jubilee Edn, 1960), London, 1960.

GH Cook, *Mediaeval Chantries and Chantry Chapels*, Phoenix House, London, 1963.

N Pevsner and D Lloyd, *The Buildings of England, Hampshire*. Penguin, London, 1967.

MF Hearn, 'Rectangular Ambulatories', *Journal of the Society of Architectural Historians*, 1971.

Royal Commission for Historical Monuments, East Dorset, vol 5, 1975.

Dr J Harvey, *The Perpendicular Style*, Batsford, 1978.

R Morris, *Cathedrals and Abbeys of England and Wales: The Building Church 600-1540*. Dent & Sons Ltd, London, 1979.

'Mediaeval Art and Architecture at Durham Cathedral', British Archaeological Association Conference Transactions for the Year 1977, Leeds, 1980. (See also, GJ Combs, *RIBA Journal* 3, Series 15 (1908), pp557-81.)

JR Forster, *Christchurch Priory*, 1985.

McGee, 'Early Vaults of St Etiènne of Beauvais', *Journal of the Society of Architectural Historians*, March 1986.

V Scully, *Architecture: The Natural and the Man Made. The Gothic Cathedral* – 'Structure', p123, 'Experience' p155, New York, 1991.

P Cave, *The Romantic Story of Christchurch*.

Royal Commission for Historical Monuments, Salisbury, vol 1.

The author wishes to apologise for any inconsistent references.